Billie Eilish
GLOBAL POP SENSATION

Amy Allison

ReferencePoint Press®

San Diego, CA

For more information, contact:
ReferencePoint Press, Inc.
PO Box 27779
San Diego, CA 92198
www.ReferencePointPress.com

LIBRARY OF CONGRESS CATALOGING-IN-PUBLICATION DATA

Names: Allison, Amy, 1956- author.
Title: Billie Eilish : global pop sensation / by Amy Allison.
Description: San Diego, CA : ReferencePoint Press, 2022. | Includes
   bibliographical references and index.
Identifiers: LCCN 2022063132 (print) | LCCN 2022063133 (ebook)
   ISBN 9781678203269 (library binding) | ISBN 9781678203276 (ebook)
Subjects: LCSH: Eilish, Billie, 2001---Juvenile literature.
Singers--United States--Biography--Juvenile literature.
Classification: LCC ML3930.E35 A55 2022 (print) | LCC ML3930.E35
   (ebook) | DDC 782.42164092 [B]--dc23
LC record available at https://lccn.loc.gov/2022063132
LC ebook record available at https://lccn.loc.gov/2022063133

CONTENTS

Gen Z Phenomenon

Rapper and record producer LL Cool J was just about to announce the Album of the Year winner at the 2020 Grammy Awards ceremony when the camera spotted nominee Billie Eilish mouthing, "Please don't let it be me."[1] Leading up to that moment, Eilish had already won three Grammys: Best New Artist, Best Pop Vocal Album (*When We All Fall Asleep, Where Do We Go?*), and Song of the Year ("Bad Guy"). Accepting the award for Song of the Year, Eilish had said, "So many other songs deserved this. . . . This is my first Grammys. I never thought this would happen in my whole life. I grew up watching them."[2]

That night the eighteen-year-old went on to win the Grammy Award for Album of the Year for *When We All Fall Asleep, Where Do We Go?*, followed by a win for Record of the Year for the single "Bad Guy." She made Grammy history by being not only the first female artist but also the youngest to sweep the four top awards: Album of the Year, Record of the Year, Song of the Year, and Best New Artist.

Representing Youth Culture

Eilish's youth distinguishes many of her achievements: the first US recording artist born in the twenty-first century to have a chart-topping song ("Bad Guy") and album (*When We All Fall Asleep, Where Do We Go?*), the youngest performer of a theme song for a James Bond film (*No Time to Die*), and in

2020, the youngest member of *Forbes* magazine's Celebrity 100, an annual ranking of the highest-paid entertainers worldwide.

Stepping up to the microphone after Eilish to accept the Song of the Year Grammy for "Bad Guy," Finneas O'Connell, Eilish's brother and cowriter of the song, said, "We just make music in a bedroom together. We still do that and they let us do that. This is to all of the kids who are making music in their bedroom today. You're gonna get one of these."[3]

Unlike pop artists partnered by their music labels with established songwriters and producers, Eilish writes and records music with Finneas in his home studio. A member of a generation that grew up in the digital age, Eilish owes her pop stardom to a boost from the music-sharing platform SoundCloud. "Only in the last decade could a teenager have a home studio with the capacity to make radio-ready recordings, distribute songs for free online, and even interact directly with her fans through her phone,"[4] noted Charlie Harding, cohost of the podcast *Switched on Pop*, in 2019.

Connecting with Fans

Having amassed a fan base before signing with a record label, Eilish is careful to personally curate her brand. She says:

> I could easily just be like, you know what, you're going to pick out my clothes, someone else will come up with my video treatments, someone else will direct them and I won't have anything to do with them. Someone else write my music, someone else produce it, and I won't say anything about it. Someone else run my Instagram. . . . But I'm not that kind of person and I'm not that kind of artist."[5]

Describing herself as a "fan type person"[6]—most famously of Justin Bieber—Eilish has been honest about the struggle, familiar to teens caught up in social media, about how much to reveal of

her life. She has been candid about wrestling with depression, self-harm, and suicidal thoughts, which are all-too-relatable to a young audience. She has also been open about having Tourette's syndrome. Tourette's causes physical tics, like involuntary head flicking and eye widening, that worsen with fatigue or stress.

Eilish's song lyrics, their obsession with death and mix of toughness and wry humor with deep sadness, connect with a generation born in the shadow of 9/11 and living in the glare of social media. Kids her age have faced cyberbullying and threats of school shootings as well as the devastations of climate change.

"People tell me at meet and greets, 'My daughter was hospitalized five times this year, and your daughter's music has been the only thing that kept her going,'" Eilish's mother, Maggie Baird, said to *Vogue* magazine. "These are girls for whom Billie is their lifeline. It's very intense."[7]

Speaking from the Heart

Before her twentieth birthday, Eilish made *Time* magazine's list of the 100 Most Influential People of 2021. Paying tribute to her in the magazine, rap artist Megan Thee Stallion recalled meeting her on Grammy night earlier that year. "She had already achieved worldwide stardom, which might make some people have airs about them, but not Billie. She was so real and laid-back, even though her personality is so big. She is a rare spirit who speaks from her heart with no pretenses," Megan Thee Stallion wrote. "One who is strong, but still learning and still growing."[8]

At the 2021 Grammy Awards ceremony, Eilish again took home the Record of the Year award, this time for her song "Everything I Wanted." However, during her acceptance speech, she argued that Megan Thee Stallion truly deserved the award. Musician and journalist Paul Zollo remarks that Eilish's attempt to relinquish her award to Megan Thee Stallion was not a hollow gesture. He writes that Eilish "learned early on a lesson many artists never learn: that being true to one's self in art and life matters more than anything, as does recognizing and empowering fellow artists."[9] Eilish's gesture reflected her generous nature and her gratitude at receiving so much acclaim as a young performer still making her way in a crowded field of up-and-coming recording artists.

> "[Billie Eilish] is a rare spirit who speaks from her heart with no pretenses."[8]
>
> —Megan Thee Stallion, rap artist

CHAPTER ONE

Bohemian Beginnings

Actors Maggie Baird and Patrick O'Connell met while performing together in a play, and they married in 1995. Their list of acting credits includes occasional roles in TV series: Baird in *Charmed* and *The X-Files* and O'Connell in *Supergirl*. Baird also has performed in the acclaimed Los Angeles–based improvisational group the Groundlings.

But by the time their daughter, Billie Eilish Pirate Baird O'Connell, was born on December 18, 2001, Baird and O'Connell were less focused on their acting careers. Along with doing voiceover work for video games, Baird taught improv and aerial classes, and O'Connell took carpentry jobs to help support their family, which already included Eilish's older brother, Finneas.

Finneas, four years older than Eilish, contributed *Pirate* to her name. *Billie* honors Eilish's maternal grandfather, William, who died a few months before her birth. Baird and McConnell chose *Eilish*, an Irish variant of *Elizabeth*, after watching a documentary about Eilish Holton, a successfully separated conjoined twin.

Home Base

Eilish grew up in a two-bedroom Craftsman-style house in Highland Park, a section of northeast Los Angeles. Highland Park is home to artists and academics, as well as to film and television production workers and other supporting players, like

Baird and O'Connell, in the entertainment industry. Music journalist Ann Powers says of the neighborhood, "It's exactly the kind of milieu where weird achievers are deeply nurtured." She adds of its influence on Eilish, "Hollywood craft and knowledge, her inheritance, is part of what makes her a prodigy, and a pop star."[10]

Eilish's brother has contrasted their unconventional childhood with the more conventional upbringing of their friends. Of their friends' eagerness to move out of their childhood homes in reaction to how they were parented, Finneas remarked to *Vogue*, "Truth be told, we never had that feeling. I think our parents never trivialized our questions and our interests."[11]

Eilish shared her childhood home not just with her parents and her brother but also with musical instruments, including three pianos, among them a grand piano her father acquired for free online. With coaching from her father, she learned to play piano as well as

> **"Our parents never trivialized our questions and our interests."**[11]
>
> —Finneas O'Connell

the ukulele. "Music was always underlying," she says. "I always sang. It was like wearing underwear: It was just always underneath whatever else you were doing."[12] Baird and O'Connell were so supportive of their children's musical activities that they never forced Eilish and Finneas to go to bed if they were making music.

Artistic Curriculum

In 1997, the year Finneas was born, the group Hanson released the hit single "MMMBop." O'Connell was convinced that homeschooling had allowed the three Hanson brothers the freedom to pursue their artistic interests. Baird's roots in Colorado, where the Columbine High School massacre took place in 1999, also played a part in her and O'Connell's decision to homeschool Eilish and Finneas. Additionally, Baird and O'Connell wanted to spend as much time as possible with their children, especially since Eilish came along relatively late in their lives: Baird at forty-two and O'Connell at forty-four.

Besides the use of everyday activities in their learning—for example, cooking to build math skills—homeschooling for Eilish and her brother involved "strewing." Their parents presented them with books, paints, and other items, along with different activities, and observed which the children gravitated toward. Eilish was drawn to singing and dancing.

Eilish's first experience singing before an audience was at homeschool talent shows. When she was six years old, her father accompanied her on the keyboards as she performed the Beatles' song "Happiness Is a Warm Gun," which cycles through different styles of rock and roll music.

At age eight, Eilish joined the Los Angeles Children's Chorus (LACC). "It's taught me all of my technique," she says. "Choir has taught me the way to protect your voice and not f**k it up because you're just screaming. Some artists just ruin their voices because they don't know any better."[13] Eilish also learned how to read and write music while with LACC. She credits the ease with which she figures out a harmony to her choral training.

Eilish grew up in a Los Angeles, California, neighborhood just 12 miles from Hollywood and its booming entertainment industry.

Also, around age eight, Eilish took ballet lessons. She hated them, though, preferring tap, which led her to hip-hop and contemporary styles of dance. By age twelve, she had been accepted into a dance troupe at the Revolution Dance Center in Montrose, California, on the outskirts of Los Angeles, and was spending up to eleven hours a week in dance class. "I have always moved in song," Eilish says. "Dance classes were just an extension of that."[14]

Eilish learned the basics of songwriting through a once-a-week class her mother taught for a co-op homeschool program, WISH, short for Workshops Investing in Socializing Homeschoolers. When given an assignment to watch a movie or TV show and write down lines she thought were promising as song hooks or titles, Eilish chose her favorite show at the time, *The Walking Dead*. "I wrote this song about the apocalypse in my mind, and it came out as a love song—a longing despair, which wasn't my intention, but it happened," Eilish recalls about the first song she "really wrote," at age eleven, titled "Fingers Crossed." Up until that time, she had composed "random stupid little things" and at age four came up with a song about falling into a black hole, though she claims that "it was really upbeat."[15]

Outsider Status

Eilish shrugs off claims that she is breaking the mold of pop stardom. It is not her intention to break molds or rules or conform to them either. "Maybe people see me as a rule-breaker because they themselves feel like they have to follow rules, and here I am not doing it. That's great, if I can make someone feel more free to do what they actually want to do instead of what they are expected to do. But for me, I never realized that I was expected to do anything," Eilish says. "Nobody told me that . . . so I did what I wanted."[16]

Eilish's mother remembers her being strong-willed from her early childhood. She would not even let her mother buckle up her car seat.

Los Angeles Children's Chorus

Since 1986 the Los Angeles Children's Chorus (LACC) has provided Los Angeles residents ages six to eighteen with a choral music education. A scholarship program ensures that families across the city's economic spectrum can fund their children's participation in LACC.

The curriculum follows an experience-based approach to learning: the experience of singing during rehearsals reinforces concepts learned in class. Besides training in reading and writing music and in basic music theory, choristers receive one-on-one vocal coaching. They also learn to interpret music from various time periods and cultures.

LACC presents a multilingual repertoire and tours nationally as well as internationally. The group performs frequently with esteemed music ensembles such as the Los Angeles Philharmonic, Hollywood Bowl Orchestra, and Los Angeles Chamber Orchestra. LACC members also perform with the Los Angeles Opera in productions that call for a children's chorus or child soloists.

LACC has been the subject of four documentaries by Oscar-winning filmmaker Freida Mock, including *Sing!* Chronicling a year in the life of the chorus, *Sing!* received an Academy Award nomination for Best Documentary Short in 2001.

Despite her independent streak, Eilish was not immune from peer pressure. "Peer pressure is real; I had some of that," she told *British GQ*. "Although because I wasn't at school and didn't know what school actually was, to a degree, I was definitely spared some of that mad bullying that goes on in hallways and so on after class."[17]

While she was not bullied, Eilish recalls feeling like an outsider at the stables where she took horseback riding lessons. To pay for her lessons, she groomed the horses and cleaned their stalls. "I didn't make any friends riding horses," she says. "Nobody wanted to be a little girl with no money at an equestrian center. Nobody."[18]

Body Insecurity

Eilish started wearing baggy clothes because she felt the need to hide her body. When you are a teenager, she explains, your body is your "deepest insecurity."[19] She recalls that she developed early: "I had boobs at nine. I got my period at 11. So my body was going faster than my brain. It's funny, because when you're a little kid, you don't think of your body at all. And all of a sudden, you look down and you're, like, whoa. What can I do to make this go away?"[20]

When she was fourteen, Eilish's body issues led her to start cutting herself. She would hide razors in her bedroom and lock herself inside the bathroom, where she would make herself bleed. According to medical professionals, self-injury is an attempt to release tension built up from anxiety and frustration. Adolescents have the highest rate of self-injurious acts of any age group, with about 17 percent admitting to committing self-harm at least once in their lives.

Whether in concert or on the red carpet, Billie Eilish is known for often wearing baggy clothing.

An end to her participation in LACC added to Eilish's sense of despair. Her failure to be accepted into the choir's elite chamber singers when she was thirteen led to her departure from the choir. "It was really emotional for me," she told *Vogue*. "I knew that if I left, everybody would form new friendships without me. When I think back to me crying about it then, I was crying about the future and what I thought it would be."[21]

Also feeding into her depression, Eilish was forced to eventually quit dance lessons after she suffered a serious physical injury at age thirteen. Performing a hip-hop move in class, she damaged the growth plate in her hip. Her hip bone separated from her hip muscles, causing persistent pain and tenderness. Such an injury happens only when a person is under age sixteen. The move had been choreographed for Eilish's older classmates, whose skill level, if not physical maturity, Eilish had achieved.

Dance Track

Eilish's injury prevented her from dancing with her troupe to a song she and Finneas recorded for the troupe's performance at a recital. Her dance instructor, Fred Diaz, had asked Eilish to contribute a song for him to choreograph for the performance.

Earlier, in October 2015, Finneas had walked into Eilish's room to tell her he had written a song for his band, the Slightlys, and he wanted to sing it for her. He thought it would suit her voice. "And I was like, 'Yeah, I know. I could hear it. I've been hearing it the entire time you've been writing it,'" Eilish recalls. "We were like three feet away from each other in our rooms, so any song either of us were writing, the other one could hear it."[22]

Once they agreed to allow Diaz to use the song, Eilish and Finneas came up with an arrangement that would fit with contemporary dance choreography. They created the track in

"[Finneas and I] were like three feet away from each other in our rooms, so any song either of us were writing, the other one could hear it."[22]

—Billie Eilish

Me & Dad Radio

On May 9, 2020, Eilish and her father, Patrick O'Connell, debuted *Me & Dad Radio* on Apple Music's Beats 1 radio station. As cohosts of the show, Eilish and O'Connell play music they have shared with each other and chat about their choices.

The practice of sharing music in the Baird-O'Connell household goes back to when Eilish and her brother, Finneas, were children, and O'Connell would make mixtapes of bands and singers he liked, including the Beatles, Linkin Park, and Avril Lavigne.

Me & Dad Radio's playlist reveals Eilish's and O'Connell's wide-ranging tastes. Selections include singer Peggy Lee's torchy 1956 cover of the song "Fever," Bob Marley and the Wailers' 1973 reggae classic "Burnin' and Lootin'," hip-hop artist Kendrick Lamar's anthem-like 2015 release "Alright," and the instrumental version of the eerie theme song from the 1990s television series *Twin Peaks*.

Me & Dad Radio lets listeners in on Eilish's decades-spanning musical references. And Eilish and her father's charmingly digressive conversations hint at how at ease they are with each other.

Finneas's bedroom, with the use of Finneas's Logic Pro X digital audio workstation.

Eilish and Finneas recorded her vocals for about a week to achieve the sound she was after. The resulting synth pop tune, "Ocean Eyes," features multiple harmonies and layers of background vocals.

Viral Hit

On November 18, 2015, Finneas put up a link to "Ocean Eyes" on the music-sharing platform SoundCloud so that Diaz could download it. Before Diaz started to choreograph to the track, "Ocean Eyes" went viral, boosted by remixes from musicians Cautious Clay, Blackbear, and Astronymyy, among others. The song quickly racked up 2.2 million SoundCloud streams.

The posting of "Ocean Eyes" on the music discovery website Hillydilly attracted even more listeners. Airplay by Jason Kramer, a DJ at the Santa Monica, California, public radio station KCRW, also expanded the song's audience.

Eilish first heard the song played in public when she was at a vegan ice cream shop with Finneas and their father. "As we were ordering, 'Ocean Eyes' started playing. I started dancing around the room because no one was in there. It was kind of surreal," she recalls. "For what you make in your little space—your bedroom, studio or whatever—to end up in some random vegan ice cream shop. For me, it was super impactful and meaningful."[23]

Next-Level Success

Through the Slightlys, Finneas had met music manager Danny Rukasin. Eilish told *Teen Vogue*, "Danny Rukasin, who is now my manager, reached out to my brother and was like, 'dude, this is going to get huge and I think you're going to need help along the way. I want to help you guys.' We were like, 'that's swag!'"[24]

Adopting a strategy suited to the streaming era, Rukasin and his management partner, Brandon Goodman, put their effort into growing Eilish's online fan base instead of pursuing Top 40 airplay for "Ocean Eyes." Goodman explains, "We didn't want it to be about a song. We never wanted anything to be bigger than Billie the artist."[25]

In January 2016 Rukasin and Goodman brokered a development deal for Eilish with Platoon. A distribution platform, Platoon offers artists services that record companies provide—such as studio time, video production, and publicity—without tying them to a long-term contract, taking a share of their song rights, or reining in their artistic control.

> "We didn't want it to be about a song. We never wanted anything to be bigger than Billie the artist."[25]
>
> —Brandon Goodman, Eilish's comanager

Eilish's Platoon deal ensured that "Six Feet Under"—the second single released by Eilish—was available on iTunes, Spotify, and Amazon. A darkly

atmospheric ballad like "Ocean Eyes," the song alludes to the death of a love affair. Finneas wrote "Six Feet Under," and Eilish created a homemade video for the song. The video, edited by Eilish's mother, features smoke balls exploding in front of a fence at Eilish's Highland Park house, with the discharge of smoke shown alternately in forward and in reverse. Eilish, then fourteen, had scored another viral hit.

Record Deal

Eilish and Finneas spent 2016 meeting with music labels. They wanted to be sure that the label they signed with was trustworthy and valued Eilish for who she was and not who they imagined she could be. Eilish makes it clear that she and Finneas were not pushed by their parents into attending any meetings. Eilish explains:

> I'm not going to let somebody be like, "This is her parents exploiting her." My parents, every day, would be like, "Billie, you know that you don't have to be doing this; we can easily just stop going to these." And I wanted to do it, I wanted to have this be my life and I wanted to be going to these meetings even though they were super boring and I was 14 and I didn't know how to talk to grownups yet.[26]

In November 2016 Eilish signed a contract with Darkroom, a partner label of Interscope Records. Interscope's roster of recording artists includes Eminem, Lady Gaga, and Lana Del Rey, an artist cited by Eilish as an influence. Darkroom envisioned a long-term career for Eilish and promised her creative freedom. "We were really lucky with the people we signed with. I mean, we were put in sessions with a bunch of random producers, random writers and artists and stuff," Eilish says. "And I think it just solidified the fact that me and Finneas work best together. I think it just made us realize that even more than we knew before."[27] Eilish understands that songs like those she and Finneas write together, which connect deeply and intimately with fans, cannot be artificially manufactured. She explains, "When we write, just us together, it's so much more raw, I guess. And straight from the heart."[28]

Eilish's creative partnership with Finneas is strongly rooted in familiarity and trust. As a teenager embarking on a music career, Eilish could count on her brother's and her parents' solid support. It was her parents' encouragement of her creativity that helped Eilish gain the musical training and confidence in her talent that made it possible for her to achieve success at an early age. She can thank her unconventional upbringing for much of her originality and authenticity as an artist—qualities that convinced representatives of the music industry to gamble on signing her.

CHAPTER TWO

Dreams and Nightmares

Eilish and Finneas spent the first half of 2017 producing a steady stream of singles, leading up to the release of an eight-track EP, *Don't Smile at Me*, on August 11. Eilish co-wrote most of the selections with Finneas, except "Ocean Eyes," and "Watch," which Finneas wrote on his own. Culture journalist Katherine Cusumano comments that Eilish's "pop influences can be heard in her playful, word-association lyrics, and her precociousness has earned her comparisons to Lorde," adding that Eilish cites "influences like Tyler, the Creator, in whose lyrics 'everything is everything.'"[29] Critics have noted the impact of trap, a style of hip-hop characterized by multilayered, percussive sound, on the production of Eilish's music.

A December 2017 reissue of *Don't Smile at Me* included "&Burn," a collaboration with the rapper Vince Staples. An expanded edition of the EP added the rhythm and blues–inflected, post-breakup tune "Bitches Broken Hearts," cowritten and coproduced by Emmit Fenn. It also included the ballad "Lovely," cowritten with the rhythm and blues artist Khalid, who performs on the track with Eilish.

Shadow Self

"Lovely," which addresses the singers' attempts to overcome depression, won a spot on the soundtrack to the second season of *13 Reasons Why*, a Netflix series dealing with teen suicide. "Bored," a song from *Don't Smile at Me* about being trapped in a toxic relationship, was featured in the series' first season.

Eilish came up with the concept for the video of "Bored," which shows her attempting to climb a seemingly limitless ladder. "The thought of being on an endless ladder in a kind of timeless, anti-gravity space where no rules apply, is just really sick to

Eilish's songs "Lovely" and "Bored" were both featured in the Netflix series 13 Reasons Why, *which aired from 2017 to 2020.*

THE TAPES WERE JUST THE BEGINNING

A NETFLIX ORIGINAL SERIES

13 REASONS WHY ▶

ALL EPISODES MAY 18 | NETFLIX

me, and goes with the concept of the song—getting nowhere in a relationship,"[30] she explains.

The bleakness at the heart of "Bellyache," the second single released from *Don't Smile at Me*, is in keeping with the dark cast to the tracks on the EP. The lyrics to "Bellyache" adopt the point of view of a psychopath. Eilish describes the song as about "getting a bellyache because you just killed a bunch of people, which you would if you just killed a bunch of people if you were human, but psychopaths don't really have those feelings. We kind of just became this character that knows they're out of their mind, but also doesn't at the same time. . . . It's fun to become somebody else or become nobody—just your imagination."[31] Recording artists Eilish admires—including Lana Del Rey, Marina and the Diamonds, Aurora, and Tyler, the Creator—also have assumed dark personas in their songs.

> "It's fun to become somebody else or become nobody—just your imagination."[31]
>
> —Billie Eilish

Headliner

In October 2017 Eilish launched her headlining Don't Smile at Me Tour in support of the EP, with dates in the United States and Canada. She started the show with the EP's opening track, "Copycat." The song, which decries wannabes, features a harsh, grunge-style bassline that gives way to a plaintive piano bridge.

Just seven months earlier, on March 4, Eilish had performed at CRSSD, a two-day electronic music festival at San Diego's Waterfront Park in her home state of California. "Like ten people showed up, which was my biggest crowd yet at the time,"[32] she recalls. Later that month she headlined Apple Music's showcase artist event at South by Southwest, a leading film, tech, and music festival held annually in Austin, Texas.

Tickets for Eilish's second headlining tour in support of *Don't Smile at Me* sold out within an hour. The Where's My Mind Tour took its name from a line in the song "Bellyache." The tour, with dates in Europe as well as the United States and Canada, launched on February 14, 2018. Music journalist Lyndsey Havens hailed Eilish's show at New York City's Bowery Ballroom as "explosive, tender, and entirely exciting. . . . It was the type of show where you're acutely aware that the artist you are currently watching will outgrow the venue they are playing almost immediately."[33]

The excitement around the Where's My Mind Tour had its downside for the sixteen-year-old Eilish. "I didn't want to be famous. I didn't want to be going on tour and missing all my friends," she recalls. "It was weird to have all these consequences and people watching me, and I didn't want it."[34] Eilish's emotional turmoil brought her close to suicide in a Berlin hotel room. Weeping while reading hateful tweets on her smartphone, she was contemplating how she would die. Prompted by her mother's concern, a visit from her tour manager pulled her back from the edge.

> "I didn't want to be famous. I didn't want to be going on tour and missing all my friends."[34]
>
> —Billie Eilish

The Real Deal

In 2018 preorders from Apple Music subscribers reached eight hundred thousand for Eilish's debut album, which dropped on March 29 of the following year. The album received critical acclaim, with *Variety* praising its "real-dealness" and admiring Eilish as "ridiculously crafty."[35] *When We All Fall Asleep, Where Do We Go?* impressed *Rolling Stone*'s Suzy Exposito as "an album full of dressed-down avant-pop with D.I.Y. immediacy and intimacy that can still hold its own amid Top 40 maximalists like Ariana Grande and Halsey."[36]

When We All Fall Asleep, Where Do We Go? took the number one spot on the year-end 2019 *Billboard* 200 albums chart. It also won Eilish and Finneas Grammy Awards for Album of the Year and Best Pop Vocal Album.

The album's success justified Eilish's refusal to record the LP at a professional studio, as her label had preferred. "We don't like studios," she told *Vogue* about her and Finneas's insistence on producing the tracks in his bedroom studio. "I hate not seeing daylight. I hate that they smell weird. I hate recording booths. I hate being far away and singing alone in a room."[37]

Creating the album in a familiar, relaxed setting no doubt allowed for the spontaneity of the segment starting it off: Eilish sucking out her Invisalign dental straightener, announcing the album, and then laughing with Finneas. "I just thought if we could start a really dark album with a moment of levity and light—not taking ourselves too seriously—it would make the rest of the album much more impactful for people,"[38] Finneas explains.

> "I just thought if we could start a really dark album with a moment of levity . . . it would make the rest of the album much more impactful."[38]
>
> —Finneas O'Connell

ASMR

Billie Eilish counts autonomous sensory meridian response (ASMR) enthusiasts among her fans. ASMR refers to the spine-tingling sensation people feel in reaction to certain triggers, most commonly whispering. For many, Eilish's close-miked vocals create a shivery sense that she is whispering in their ear.

Besides her hushed, whispery singing, Eilish's music incorporates elements of ASMR such as crisp, rhythmic sounds—for example, scraping, snapping, and clicking. On Eilish's debut album, the track "You Should See Me in a Crown" opens with the sound of knife sharpening, while amplified finger snaps are heard in "Bad Guy" and a staple gun in "Bury a Friend."

Following the release of *When We All Fall Asleep, Where Do We Go?*, ASMR practitioner and Eilish fan Gibi produced an ASMR read-through of the album commissioned by Eilish's label. Gibi, whose YouTube channel boasts over 2 million subscribers, recommends listening to Eilish's music through headphones: "You can catch all of the tiny sounds and noises, so it feels extremely immersive. Compared to other music that is a little more flat, I feel like Billie's music is 3D."

Meredith Geaghan-Breiner and Justin Gmoser, "Transcript: Billie Eilish Just Won International Female Solo Artist at the BRIT Awards. Here's How She Incorporates ASMR into Her Music," *Insider*, May 11, 2021. www.insider.com.

Perfectionism

The second track on *When We All Fall Asleep, Where Do We Go?* scored Eilish her first Hot 100 number one song. The popularity of "Bad Guy," which won two Grammy Awards in 2020, for Song of the Year and Record of the Year, shocked Eilish. She had expected "Bad Guy," cowritten with Finneas, to flop because the song's chorus lacks a catchy hook.

A snappy synth hook in "Bad Guy" references both a tune from the video game *Plants vs. Zombies* and the theme song for the Disney Channel series *Wizards of Waverly Place*. The track also incorporates the sound of crosswalk signals in Sydney, Australia, captured by Eilish on her smartphone.

As evidence of Eilish's perfectionism, she recorded the phrase "white shirt" that begins the song hundreds of times until she was satisfied with her enunciation. She also recorded thirty-four takes of the deflating "duh" that recurs in the track.

The surreal music video for "Bad Guy" depicts the tangled power dynamics teased out by the song's lyrics. Sequences include Eilish smearing blood from her nose over her face and sitting cross-legged on the back of a guy doing push-ups. The video won a 2019 MTV Video Music Award for Best Editing the same evening that Eilish took home VMAs for Best New Artist and Push Artist of the Year, which honors a breakthrough performer. In November 2020, to celebrate the video having achieved 1 billion streams, YouTube produced "Infinite Bad Guy," a music video using artificial intelligence to randomly present thousands of fans' covers, lip synchs, and dance routines to the track.

A Visual Artist

The third track on *When We All Fall Asleep, Where Do We Go?* takes its title, "Xanny," from the slang term for the drug Xanax. Prescribed to improve mood, Xanax can be dangerously addictive when taken recreationally.

Eilish credits recording artist Feist as an influence for the song's velvety-smooth verses. The chorus, by contrast, is dominated

by a heavy, distorted bassline, meant to be as discomforting as breathing in secondhand smoke. Eilish and Finneas, who do not do drugs or smoke, wrote "Xanny" to evoke the misery they have felt at parties in the company of substance-using friends.

The unnerving music video for "Xanny" shows Eilish sitting impassively while cigarettes are put out on her face until she walks away, followed by cigarette smoke filling the frame. The video earned Eilish a 2020 VMA nomination for Best Direction. "I am a very visual person, and music videos have always been my favorite form of artistry, ever since I was a kid," Eilish says. "Since the beginning, almost all of my videos were my own ideas. I just didn't know that I could direct them."[39]

Night Terrors and Monsters

Eilish has been open about her bouts with sleep paralysis and nightmares, to which she owes the creation of the tenth track on the album, the electro-pop "Bury a Friend." The album title *When We*

Blohsh

Billie Eilish has shown a flair for fashion since her early teens, when she started making her own clothing. She would cut up clothes she bought at Target and sew them into original outfits. She once created a shirt out of an Ikea shopping bag.

In 2018 Eilish launched a unisex clothing and accessories brand, which has its own online store and Instagram account. Eilish first drew the brand's Blohsh logo, a slightly off-balance abstract human figure, when she was fourteen.

Eilish was hands-on in designing the initial collection. "I did it really janky," she says. "I'd download a picture of a white hoodie off Google, and then I'd color it myself and put the designs where I wanted them."

Eilish has stayed involved in the design process for her Blohsh merch, which has grown to include a kid's line. A neon green hoodie from the line sold out within hours of being posted.

Quoted in Brooke Mazurek, "Billie Eilish on How Her 'Janky' Designs Inspired Her Merch Line Blohsh," *Billboard*, March 22, 2019. www.billboard.com.

All Fall Asleep, Where Do We Go? is taken from a line in the song, cowritten with Finneas. Eilish has in fact attributed all the tracks on the LP to her experiences with disordered sleep and lucid dreaming.

In "Bury a Friend," Eilish sings from the perspective of the mythic scary monster under the bed. "Anything could be the monster—it could be someone you love so much that it's taking over your life,"[40] she explains. Bone-chilling sound effects such as a dental drill, staple gun, and breaking glass, as well distortions of Eilish's vocals, contribute to the eeriness of the track.

In the unsettling music video for "Bury a Friend," latex-gloved hands prod Eilish and inject her with needles. Similarly nightmarish videos were created for the LP's fourth track, "You Should See Me in a Crown," and the seventh, "When the Party's Over." In the video for "When the Party's Over," Eilish ghoulishly weeps black tears. The video directed by the acclaimed Japanese artist Takashi Murakami for "You Should See Me in a Crown" features an anime likeness of Eilish who morphs into a monstrous spider-like creature and terrorizes a town.

Sounding an Alarm

The music video for "All the Good Girls Go to Hell"—the fifth track on *When We All Fall Asleep, Where Do We Go?*—adopts the horror movie spookiness of the LP's other videos to relay a warning about global climate change. The video starts with Eilish sprouting wings and flying before she crashes down onto an oil spill. Her body and wings now heavy with oil, she roams a burning landscape. Eventually her wings, too, catch fire.

Eilish's determination to limit the use of digital visual effects, such as computer-generated imagery, for her videos paid off when "All the Good Girls Go to Hell" was nominated for a 2020 VMA for Best Visual Effects. To create the video, she endured dangling off a crane and having a pair of 15-foot (4.6 m) prop wings strapped to her back. The wings weighed 40 pounds (18 kg) even before the application of the gooey substance, which added to their heft.

"All the Good Girls Go to Hell" also earned a 2020 VMA nomination for Video for Good, an award for artists who address relevant social topics in their videos. Eilish released the video on September 4, 2019, timed to the climate strikes inspired by activist Greta Thunberg. The strikes were scheduled for September 20 to 27 in anticipation of the United Nations hosting the 2019 Climate Action Summit on September 29. The day of the video's release, Eilish called for her Instagram followers to make their voices heard and take to the streets to help goad the summit toward action in the fight against global climate change.

On November 24, 2019, for her debut on the American Music Awards, Eilish sang "All the Good Girls Go to Hell" wearing a T-shirt emblazoned with the message "No Music on a Dead Planet." That evening she won in the categories New Artist of the Year and Favorite Artist–Alternative Rock.

Confronting Controversy

In "Wish You Were Gay," the album's sixth track, Eilish counts down the ways someone she has feelings for does not share them. The song was inspired by Eilish's unrequited crush on a friend in real life. To feel less personally rejected, she imagined the guy was gay. The guy did in fact come out to her as gay a couple of months after she and Finneas wrote the song.

The release of "I Wish You Were Gay" as a single on March 4, 2019, provoked members of the LGBTQ community to accuse Eilish of queerbaiting, which is a marketing technique of hinting at same-sex relationships to gain an audience. Eilish denied the charge, claiming she never meant to offend anyone, while also avoiding criticism of her detractors. "It's not anyone's place to tell somebody that their being offended is not correct, you know?" she told NPR. "It's, like, that's a thing that you can't control. And if somebody doesn't feel OK with something, then you have to respect that and understand that and not try to fight that."[41]

To demonstrate her support of the LGBTQ community, Eilish donated a portion of the proceeds from her merchandise over a forty-eight-hour period to the Trevor Project, a suicide and crisis prevention nonprofit serving LGBTQ youth.

Creating Links

Eilish and Finneas intend for the titles of the last three tracks on *When We All Fall Asleep, Where Do We Go?*—"Listen Before I Go," "I Love You," "Goodbye"—to form a sentence. The linkage supports Eilish and Finneas's goal of making the album cohesive and not just an arbitrary collection of songs. The goal is consistent with Eilish's claim that all the tracks on the LP relate to what happens when you fall asleep.

Also demonstrating interconnectedness, both "Listen Before I Go" and "I Love You" include disquieting ambient sounds. Ambulance sirens blare at the end of "Listen Before I Go," which alludes to a suicide attempt. The faint voice of an airline attendant

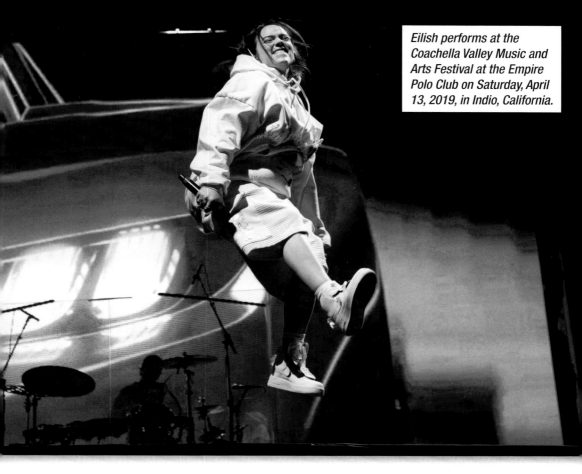

Eilish performs at the Coachella Valley Music and Arts Festival at the Empire Polo Club on Saturday, April 13, 2019, in Indio, California.

speaking about emergency exits and the roar of a plane taking off are heard in "I Love You."

The LP's final track, "Goodbye," borrows a line from each of the LP's songs. "That was Billie's idea, and I just thought it was really cool," Finneas says, adding that he "layered in, really quietly, clips of all the songs on the album and played them backwards. To us, the motif would be when you grow up listening to a tape and at the end, you reverse the tape to go back to the beginning of the song."[42]

Reimagining a Dream

Eilish's debut at the famed Coachella Valley Music and Arts Festival in Indio, California, kicked off the When We All Fall Asleep World Tour to promote her debut album. Slated for a late-night slot at the Outdoor Theater on April 13, 2019, Eilish drew a crowd that camped out before her set time. Technical difficulties with the onstage screens and a delayed start that forced her to cut two songs from the set list failed to dampen her fans' enthusiasm. Singing along to her songs, the audience came to her aid when she blanked on lyrics to "All the Good Girls Go to Hell," which only endeared her to them to more. Eilish, nevertheless, was distraught over her performance.

Known for her frenetic jumping and dancing onstage, Eilish frequently performed in pain while on tour. Injuries such as shin splints, torn ligaments, and sprained ankles dogged her. The demands of touring, made worse by attacks of loneliness, tormented her up until the summer. Sessions with a therapist and the presence of her best friend, Zoe Donahoe, on tour helped ease her anguish.

In the fall of 2019, with the tour winding down, she and Finneas finished writing a song they had begun the previous year based on a dream of Eilish's about stepping off the Golden Gate Bridge. Concerned about his sister's emotional fragility at the time, Finneas had been uncomfortable with the lyrics' bleak fatalism, and they shelved the song. "As soon as we decided that it was going to be more about not giving in to your bad thoughts and just being there for each other, I think that was really fun and satisfying,"[43] Eilish says regarding "Everything I Wanted." The song earned her and Finneas a Record of the Year award at the 2021 Grammy Awards ceremony.

In pursuit of a dream to succeed as a recording artist, Eilish mined her nightmares for songwriting gold. With her debut album, she achieved success on her own terms. Facing her fears and meeting challenges such as physical injuries and emotional distress while on tour helped Eilish develop resilience, which has served her well in contending with the pressures of fame.

CHAPTER THREE

Growth Factor

On December 18, 2019, Billie Eilish turned eighteen. She and guests at her birthday party celebrated with a bouncy house, piñata, and home-baked vegan chocolate birthday cake with vegan cream cheese frosting.

Eilish's eighteenth birthday marked her independence from her parents' legal guardianship in pursuit of her music career. At eighteen she was legally an adult, able to sign documents such as contracts on her own. Moving past this milestone, Eilish has remained close to her parents and appreciative of their nurture of her and her talent.

Bond Song

On February 9, 2020, Eilish performed during the in-memoriam segment of the Academy Awards ceremony, which pays tribute to deceased members of the film industry. She sang a cover of the Beatles song "Yesterday" accompanied by Finneas on piano.

Eilish's rendition of the frequently covered song earned her mostly positive reviews, including an A grade in *USA Today*'s "Brutally Honest Rankings of the Oscars 2020 Musical Performances." Eilish, however, expressed dissatisfaction with her performance. She explained that singing before an audience of movie stars made her unusually nervous.

Days after her performance at the Oscars, Eilish claimed another achievement in the film industry. On February 14 the theme song she and Finneas created for the James Bond film *No Time to Die* was released. The somber, melancholy ballad plays over the film's title sequence, which follows a cold open, or initial scene.

For years the siblings had wanted to write a Bond song and even played around with possible melodies. They started composing a theme for real in the fall of 2019, soon after receiving the initial scene from the film script. Once Finneas came up with the theme's piano motif, he and Eilish wrote and recorded "No Time to Die" in three days during the When We All Fall Asleep World Tour.

In the tradition of Bond songs, Eilish belts the final note of "No Time to Die." When singers belt, they use their chest, or speaking, voice to achieve a deeper, stronger tone when singing high notes, which generally fall in the range of their airier head voice—in which the notes they sing are felt as vibrations inside the head. Finneas has acknowledged that a younger Eilish would have lacked the training or stamina to perform the technique.

Eilish and Finneas were rewarded for their efforts on the Bond song. In 2021 "No Time to Die" won them a Grammy Award for Best Song Written for Visual Media. And in 2022 "No Time to Die" also scored them an Academy Award nomination for Best Original Song.

Lockdown

Eilish's Where Do We Go? World Tour kicked off on March 9, 2020, in Miami and ended after the third show, on March 12, in Raleigh, North Carolina. On March 16 the announcement came that the remaining dates of the tour in North America were postponed due to the COVID-19 pandemic, followed by an announcement on May 13 postponing shows in South America, Europe, and Asia. In December the tour was officially canceled, and ticket holders were promised a full refund.

Forced into lockdown after three years of a packed schedule, Eilish found herself with unexpected time off. She kept busy fostering a couple of pit bull puppies, Jem and Boo, named after characters in the novel *To Kill a Mockingbird*, and adopted a full-

Eilish and brother Finneas attend the premiere of the James Bond film No Time to Die, *for which Eilish performed the theme song, in London on September 28, 2021.*

grown gray pit bull she named Shark. She also lent financial and social media backing to Support + Feed, a nonprofit launched by her mother in partnership with restaurants at the start of lockdown to supply plant-based meals to Los Angeles residents experiencing food insecurity; the program has since spread to New York City, Philadelphia, and Washington, DC.

About a month into lockdown, Eilish's mother suggested that Eilish and Finneas follow a weekly schedule. Three days a week Eilish would drive to the house Finneas had bought the year before in the Los Feliz neighborhood of Los Angeles, and they would write music together and play video games.

On April 3, 2020, starting off their new schedule, Eilish and Finneas wrote the song "My Future." After a couple of months, they caught on to the fact that they were creating an album.

Gift of Change

With a sophomore album, artists often feel pressure to compete with the success of a best-selling debut. Eilish upended this expectation. Free of deadlines and meetings with her record label, she felt less pressure, not more, than during the creation of *When We All Fall Asleep, Where Do We Go?* Her increasing confidence and maturity helped make the difference.

No longer tortured by songwriting, Eilish cowrote all the songs on the new LP, *Happier Than Ever*. "It's been awesome as a big brother to see her become more confident and feel more owner-

A poster in Cardiff, Wales, advertises Billie Eilish's sophomore album, Happier Than Ever.

ship and just to be more excited than I've ever seen her about the music that we're making,"[44] Finneas told *Rolling Stone*.

The lyrics to the songs Eilish was cowriting with Finneas reflect her growing maturity. In "Getting Older," the album's opening track, Eilish assesses herself with clear-eyed objectivity. While confessing to her tendency to indulge in self-pity, she also declares her acceptance of responsibility and claims satisfaction with how she is aging. "My Future," the fourth song on the album, also expresses Eilish's increasing self-possession. In a musing, subdued tone, she sings about getting to know herself better and being in love with her future.

> "It's been awesome as a big brother to see [Billie] become more confident and feel more ownership . . . about the music that we're making,"[44]
>
> —Finneas O'Connell

Also evolving were Eilish's vocals. She credits the change, including a greater suppleness to her voice, to the influence of jazz vocalists from the 1950s and 1960s like Julie London and Peggy Lee. "I've grown so much and gotten so much better in my voice, it's crazy to think about," she explains. "I think change is one of the best gifts in the world."[45]

Time to Reflect

The pandemic's pause on Eilish's hectic schedule gave her time to reflect on the huge shifts in her life since becoming a pop sensation. Songs she and Finneas were writing for *Happier Than Ever* grapple with fame and desire and the costs they exact. "When you're happier than ever, that doesn't mean you're the happiest that anyone's ever been. It means you're happier than you were before,"[46] Eilish explains. On the cover of the album, a lone teardrop shows on Eilish's face. *Happier Than Ever* earned Eilish Grammy nominations for Album of the Year and Best Pop Vocal Album.

In *Happier Than Ever,* Eilish explores such familiar themes as the fallout from fame and loss of innocence in a way that feels bracing and new. "She's not the first rookie pop star who's ever responded with an album about the down side of fame. But nothing on *Happier Than Ever* feels like a cliché," writes music journalist Rob Sheffield in *Rolling Stone*. "It's a dark, painful, confessional album where she's choosing not to settle into the role of America's beloved kooky kid sister. She's got trauma to figure out and secrets to share, but she's not watering it down for anyone."[47]

Traumas faced in the album's songs include a breakup, abuse, and the loss of privacy. The spoken-word piece "Not My Responsibility," the album's ninth track, rebukes the sexualizing of women's bodies and body shaming. In May 2020 Eilish released a short film for "Not My Responsibility," clips of which had been shown during her Where Do We Go? World Tour before it shut down. The film begins with Eilish standing in darkness. She is heard in voiceover questioning sexist attitudes toward her while she removes layers of her clothing, starting with a hoodie. As she peels off a tank top, appearing in just her bra, she sinks into a black tarlike liquid. "I felt very motivated to do it," she says of the film. "Although, of course, the *Daily Mail* headlines the next day ran 'Billie strips to her bra in new tour visuals'. I thought, 'Are you actually deadass?' How predictable."[48]

The album's tenth track, "OverHeated," also slams body shaming. In 2020, after a photo of her in a form-fitting tank top was posted online, Eilish contended with cyberbullying about her physical appearance. "I think it was just a moment of being really pissed off as a young woman in the public eye,"[49] she says about the song.

Backlash

Just as Eilish can no longer appear in public without scrutiny, her presence online and in the news media has opened her up to attack. In June 2021 she responded to a TikTok video edit of clips showing her mocking Asian accents and using the racist epithet *chink*. She apologized on Instagram for mouthing a term from a song lyric when she was in her early teens that she professes she did not know at the time was derogatory.

Eilish had stumbled into controversy a year earlier for remarks she made in *Vogue* magazine. Drawing a distinction between storytelling in songs and lying, she was quoted as saying, "There are tons of songs where people are just lying. There's a lot of that in rap right now, from people that I know who rap. It's like, 'I got my AK-47, and I'm . . . like, what? You don't have a gun. 'And all my bitches. . . .' I'm like, which bitches? That's posturing, and that's

Cover of *Vogue*

Displaying her signature acid-green-streaked hair, Eilish appeared on the cover of the March 2020 issue of *Vogue*, a coup for the fashion-conscious teen. Three separate covers were shot, each by a different photographer. A fourth, digital cover was drawn by Nastya Kovtun, a sixteen-year-old fan of Eilish's living in Russia. Kovtun is the youngest person to date to create a *Vogue* digital cover.

The magazine commissioned portraits of Eilish from Kovtun and another fan, US-based twenty-year-old Kaylee Yang, both recommended by Eilish. Kovtun's and Yang's drawings, which appear on the inside pages of the print magazine, show Eilish wearing the same Louis Vuitton dress. In Kovtun's color portrait, Eilish gazes off into the distance, while in Yang's black-and-white hyperrealistic drawing, Eilish stares straight at the viewer.

Because she does not speak or read English, Kovtun uses software to translate Eilish's lyrics into Russian so she can understand them. Kovtun credits Eilish with inspiring her to pursue drawing further at a time when Kovtun was feeling lost about what to do with her life. "I haven't met anyone who has influenced me and what I draw as much as she did," Kovtun says of Eilish.

Quoted in Liana Satenstein, "Meet Billie Eilish Fan Artists Nastya Kovtun and Kaylee Yang," *Vogue*, February 3, 2020. www.vogue.com.

not what I'm doing."[50] While called out on Twitter for her White privilege and naivete, Eilish is no hater of rap, having credited Childish Gambino as well as Tyler, the Creator as inspirations.

Two years earlier, in 2018, Eilish faced backlash when she publicly paid tribute to a rapper she was friends with, known as XXXTentacion, following his murder. XXXTentacion's trial for a domestic abuse charge was pending at the time, and Eilish—despite her own history of abuse, alluded to throughout *Happier Than Ever*—was accused of being an apologist for abusive behavior.

Eilish has acknowledged the dilemma of wanting to live privately while also wanting to express herself freely to her fans. With her budding maturity has come greater objectivity about the repercussions of fame. She says:

> I wish that I could tell the fans everything I think and feel and it wouldn't live on the internet forever. And be spoken about and called problematic, or called whatever . . . anybody wants to call any thoughts that a human has. The other sad thing is that they don't actually know me. And I don't really know them, but obviously we're connected. The problem is you feel like you know somebody, but you don't.[51]

Invasion of Privacy

"Therefore I Am," the second song released as a stand-alone single from *Happier Than Ever*, takes a swipe at consumers and perpetrators of online gossip about Eilish, who presume they know her well enough to dictate how she should dress or act. "I grew up with the internet, so it's not a new thing, which is kind of trash, but it's also like, it is what it is. The thing that's scary is that anybody can say anything and everyone might believe them," Eilish says. "The whole internet is very gullible because they want to hear drama."[52]

"The whole internet is very gullible because they want to hear drama."[52]

—Billie Eilish

The song's title, "Therefore I Am," refers to a statement by the seventeenth-century philosopher René Descartes, translated from the Latin *cogito, ergo sum* as "I think, therefore I am." In other words, individuals' consciousness of their thoughts proves their existence. Eilish alone is aware of her thoughts, assuring her the right to self-determination.

The electropop track may sound jaunty and upbeat, but Eilish has suffered harassment from fans and stalkers. In 2019, after the address of her family's Highland Park home leaked online, strangers would randomly show up at the house. For a while, a bodyguard slept in the living room.

In June 2020 Eilish initiated a restraining order against a trespasser who repeatedly dropped by the Baird-O'Connell home. The following year, in March 2021, Eilish was granted a restraining order against a stalker who reportedly camped outside a school across the street from the house. According to court documents, he would speak to Eilish when he saw her and gesture in her direction, making a throat-slitting motion, which she interpreted as his intending her harm.

Eilish hints that her efforts to preserve her privacy have extended to her love life in "NDA," *Happier Than Ever*'s thirteenth track. "NDA" presents a dark take on dealing with romance when a person is a celebrity. Mixing bitterness and self-aware humor, Eilish sings about having a hookup sign an NDA—an abbreviation for "nondisclosure agreement"—to ensure his silence.

Abuse of Power

A reference to physical abuse in "NDA" alludes to Eilish's struggle with victimization in her romantic relationships. The album's fifteenth track, the Grammy-nominated, cathartic breakup song "Happier Than Ever," references emotional abuse. The trauma of abuse takes center stage in the acoustic ballad "Your Power," the twelfth track on the LP. The song's lyrics directly address an abuser who has taken advantage of the singer while pleading ignorance about her age.

Although Eilish has asserted the reality of what she sings about in "NDA," she has avoided revealing details, claiming that the lyrics are open to interpretation. Similarly, she insists that "Your Power" is not based on a single situation. While disclosing that some lines are about her life and others are about incidents she has witnessed, she discourages speculation when it comes to specifics. She understands that the exploitation of young women and girls is insidious as well as widespread. She says:

> It doesn't matter who you are, what your life is, your situation, who you surround yourself with, how strong you are, how smart you are. You can always be taken advantage of. That's a big problem in the world of domestic abuse or statutory rape—girls that were very confident and strong-willed finding themselves in situations where they're like, "Oh my god, I'm the victim here?" And it's so embarrass-

ing and humiliating and demoralising to be in that position of thinking you know so much and then you realise, I'm being abused right now.[53]

Eilish directed the video for "Your Power," released along with the song on April 28, 2021. The video shows Eilish perched on a mountainside as an 80-pound (36.3 kg) anaconda slithers over her body and eventually wraps around her. In September 2021 "Your Power" won Eilish a VMA for Video for Good.

Love Hormone

Advancing into womanhood, Eilish explores sexuality and sexual desire with frankness as well as playfulness in *Happier Than Ever*.

Instagram Red Flags

Billie Eilish is far from the only teenage consumer of social media who has dealt with emotional distress over body image issues. In September 2021 the *Wall Street Journal* published an article revealing how Facebook's own research shows that Instagram posts are harmful to a significant percentage of users, particularly teenage girls. The article's authors based their reporting on internal documents they had obtained. "We make body image issues worse for one in three teen girls," noted a 2019 slide presentation summarizing research conducted by Facebook. In a study of teens in the United States and United Kingdom, Facebook—which acquired Instagram in 2012—found that more than 40 percent of users of the photo- and video-sharing app who said they felt unattractive also said their dissatisfaction began on the app.

Additionally, researchers found that teens suffering emotional fallout from their Instagram use feel helpless regarding logging off. "Teens told us that they don't like the amount of time they spend on the app but feel like they have to be present," one researcher reported. "They often feel 'addicted' and know that what they're seeing is bad for their mental health but feel unable to stop themselves."

Quoted in Georgia Wells et al., "Facebook Knows Instagram Is Toxic for Teen Girls, Company Documents Show," *Wall Street Journal*, September 14, 2021. www.wsj.com.

In the LP's sixteenth track, the ballad "Male Fantasy," she distracts herself with pornography after a breakup, then considers how pornography propagates the fantasy that women's bodies exist to please men, a fantasy incompatible with genuine love. Eilish has publicly voiced regret at watching porn when she was a pre-teen, saying it led her to misunderstand what she could consent to during sex and distorted her view of what a woman's body is supposed to look like.

Not that all fantasy is harmful. Track number three, the sensual, Latin jazz–tinged "Billie Bossa Nova," imagines a touring pop star's evasion of the paparazzi to pursue a steamy love affair.

In the techno dance track "Oxytocin"—the album's tenth selection—the singer asserts her sexual attraction to a lover and her expectation, edging toward possessiveness, that he never leave her. The song's title refers to the hormone that regulates sexual activity as well as attachment.

"I write songs with my brother, and we kind of have to plug our ears when we're writing about desire for other people because we're . . . siblings," Eilish explains about creating such songs with Finneas. "The thing is, we're very open about both of our lives, so it's not weird, really. It's just fun. It's songwriting and it's storytelling. We just have to think about the art of it."[54]

Eilish's artistic as well as personal development has not come without growing pains. She has been battered by social media storms whipped up by scrutiny of her public statements and physical appearance. Additionally, her song lyrics are probed for clues to painful episodes in her life she has chosen to keep private. A lack of privacy dogs her, even as she has remained determined to live life and create art without limits set by anyone but her.

CHAPTER FOUR

Power-Up

In 2021, on the cusp of moving beyond her teen years, Billie Eilish was experimenting with different looks as well as expanding her brand. She collaborated with iconic labels such as Nike and Fender, published a book, and was featured in a full-length documentary in addition to a concert film. She also leaned into speaking out and acting on behalf of issues she cares about, such as sustainability and animal welfare.

Pinup Look

Customarily performing in loose-fitting skatewear and oversized matching jackets and pants, Eilish drew praise for not appearing sexualized, in contrast to female pop stars who perform in skimpy, skin-baring outfits. But on the cover and inside pages of the June 2021 issue of *British Vogue*, Eilish is shown wearing revealing, form-fitting clothes, including corsets and a catsuit. The corsetry was in fact her idea. Responding to the social media furor over her display of sensuality, she said, "Showing your body and showing your skin—or not—should not take any respect away from you. . . . It's about taking that power back, showing it off and not taking advantage with it. I'm not letting myself be owned anymore."[55] She has affirmed that the look was specific to the *British Vogue* photoshoot, rather than a shift in her style, which she insists on having agency over.

Eilish took inspiration for her glamorous, curvaceous appearance in the photoshoot from classic pinup looks of the mid-twentieth century, just as she has attributed the sound and feel of her album *Happier Than Ever* to vocalists of the era. The color and style of Eilish's hair underwent a transformation inspired by the same period, though with an updated softening of the look. Eilish officially showed off her new tresses in March 2021 on Instagram, helping stoke demand for the hair color, dubbed "reel blonde." The post received 1 million likes in just six minutes.

Eilish's transition from her then identifiable jet black and acid-green hair required four separate dye sessions over six weeks. Until the dye job was complete, Eilish wore a custom hairpiece in public, though before the hairpiece arrived, she donned the wig from a Billie Eilish Halloween costume she bought on Amazon. At the time, fans raised suspicions she was wearing a wig, noting that the part in her hair was off. On TikTok, one fan presented an eighteen-part investigation into the issue.

Before the year was out, so was Eilish's blond hair color. On December 2 she posted a selfie on Instagram that showed her as a brunette.

Gala Cochair

On September 13, 2021, Eilish appeared in glam mode for her debut at the Metropolitan Museum of Art's Costume Institute Gala (commonly called the Met Gala) in New York City. She wore an off-the-shoulder corseted tulle ballgown in peach from the Oscar de la Renta fashion house. She had provided the design team at Oscar de la Renta with images of mid-twentieth-century Hollywood icons Grace Kelly and Marilyn Monroe as inspirations for the look she was after.

The look suited the theme of the gala, *In America: A Lexicon of Fashion*, a salute to influential American designers. Each year the Met Gala shares a theme with the latest exhibit at the Costume Institute, for which the gala serves as a fund-raiser. Eilish was among the gala's cochairs—at nineteen years old, she became the youngest cochair in the history of the event. Her duties as cochair included helping plan the guest list, decor, and menu, and for the first time ever, the gala served only vegan meals.

Eilish showcased a new, glamorous look for the Met Gala in New York City on Monday, September 13, 2021. The gala has a new theme each year, and she adjusted her wardrobe for the event.

Eilish also made history by presenting Oscar de la Renta with a condition for wearing one of its dresses to the gala: that the company no longer use fur in its designs. Aware of Eilish's clout as an influencer of youth culture, the fashion house pledged to go fur-free.

More Merch

Banking on the popularity of her brand, Eilish has expanded the list of products associated with her name. She has not only collaborated with iconic labels but also added to her own line of merch.

In September 2021 Eilish teamed up with Fender to release a signature ukulele. The ukulele was the first musical instrument Eilish learned to play and write songs on. For fans wanting to go electric, the acoustic instrument features a preamp.

Sibling Music Acts

Plenty of sibling acts have achieved pop music stardom, including the pop-rock groups the Bee Gees, Hanson, and Haim. Those acts consist solely of brothers (the Bee Gees and Hanson) or sisters (Haim). Rarer are brother-sister acts.

One of the most famous brother-sister acts in pop music prior to Billie Eilish and Finneas O'Connell was Richard and Karen Carpenter, known as the Carpenters. In the 1970s the Carpenters had ten gold singles, meaning each had sold 500,000 copies. Serving as producer, arranger, keyboard player, harmony vocalist, and frequent songwriter, Richard was the Carpenters' predominant musical force, despite the invaluable contribution of Karen's vocals to their sound.

Karen died at age thirty-two, never having fully recovered from anorexia nervosa. She developed the eating disorder from pressure to appear slender, worsened by feelings of powerlessness, given her brother's dominant role in the Carpenters.

Unlike Karen and Richard Carpenter, Eilish and Finneas enjoy a collaborative creative relationship. When asked in 2021 why the two are billed as a solo artist under her name when he cowrote all the songs on the album *Happier Than Ever*, Finneas said, "It's her life. It's all her world. I'm helping her articulate that, but it's really her experiences that she lived through."

Quoted in Brittany Spanos, "Billie Eilish and the Pursuit of Happiness," *Rolling Stone*, June 17, 2021. www.rollingstone.com.

Also in September, Nike launched two pairs of Air Jordan sneaker styles designed in partnership with Eilish. An Air Jordan 1 KO in green pays tribute to her once green-streaked hair, while an Air Jordan 15 in beige references her blonde look. The sneakers, which are manufactured with more than 20 percent recycled materials, are 100 percent animal product–free. In December news broke of an Eilish collaboration with Nike on a pair of Air Force 1 Highs.

In November 2021 Eilish debuted a fragrance, Eilish. The eau de parfum features notes of vanilla, cocoa, mandarin, and musk.

Scents associated with the color amber have long appealed to Eilish, who has synesthesia, meaning she is able to experience one sense through another. For Eilish, the fragrance feels sensual as well as reminiscent of Christmastime. She admits to being sentimental and intends for her signature perfume to evoke nostalgia. The bottle's shape represents Eilish's favorite parts of the human body: the collarbone, neck, and chest. Made with clean ingredients—meaning they are safe for people and the environment—the fragrance is also cruelty-free. Eilish's commitment to producing cruelty-free products contributed to People for the Ethical Treatment of Animals naming her its 2021 Person of the Year.

Photo Album Memoir

Eilish offers fans a glimpse into her life in a book of photographs released May 11, 2021. Titled *Billie Eilish*, the book is a kind of visual memoir. Eilish wrote the photo captions as well as the introduction to the book, and she curated and arranged the images, which number in the hundreds. Describing the narration supplied by Eilish's captions as "unpretentious, sometimes to a fault," *Los Angeles Times* reviewer Rich Juzwiak notes, "Social media's grip on culture has made it socially acceptable for everyone, celebrity or not, to be perpetually telling their life story (or some spit-shined version of it) as it unfolds."[56]

The photos in the book—shot by Eilish, Finneas, their parents, friends, members of Eilish's team, and photographers from around the world—are laid out chronologically. The very first photo shows Eilish's mother while pregnant with her, posing with four-year-old Finneas in front of a Christmas tree. Photos such as those of Eilish celebrating a birthday or hanging out with friends are typical of snapshots seen in any family scrapbook, while others, showing Eilish at video shoots or backstage at performance venues, are more in keeping with the photo archives of a pop star.

In her introduction to the book, Eilish talks about growing up wishing to be a photographer and about loving to look through her family's photo albums. "If there's anything I want you to take away from this book, I think it's that we're all just our three-year-old selves," she writes. "No one isn't annoying, nobody isn't cringey at a certain age. No one doesn't go through different phases."[57]

Billie Eilish: In Her Own Words, a companion audiobook sold separately, provides commentary from Eilish and her parents. The family offers anecdotes and context for the photos in the print book.

Documentary Film Star

Since childhood, Eilish has loved being on camera and watching videos of herself. Eilish's mother, Maggie Baird, recalls that Eilish's first steps at ten months old were captured on video because when she saw the camera directed at her, she reached for it and walked toward Baird as Baird backed up holding the camera.

Still, Eilish found it hard to watch a cut of *Billie Eilish: The World's a Little Blurry*, the two-hour, twenty-minute documentary film about her that premiered February 26, 2021, on Apple TV+. The subtitle *The World's a Little Blurry* refers to a line in the song "Ilomilo" from Eilish's debut album, *When We All Fall Asleep, Where Do We Go?* The film follows Eilish from 2018 into early 2020 touring, performing, and creating music for the album with Finneas, as well as struggling with a romantic relationship. Ultimately, she has come to appreciate how watching the film has given her a new perspective on experiences that were painful at the time. "I was going through hell in certain parts of my life, and I had no idea anyone was seeing it," she says, adding that it would be "amazing" if "you could rewatch those parts of your life from a different perspective. And I did it!"[58]

Directed by Oscar-nominated documentary filmmaker R.J. Cutler, *Billie Eilish: The World's a Little Blurry* goes behind the scenes, with Eilish fulfilling pop star obligations like interviews and meet-and-greets, including an awkward post-concert gathering of record company VIPs, after which she laments that she is not allowed one bad moment. She is also seen in situations familiar to teens throughout the United States, such as visiting the Department of Motor Vehicles for her driver's license and bearing with her father's safe-driving advice before she drives solo for the first time. She achieved this milestone in her beloved matte black Dodge Challenger, which she has named Dragon.

The documentary Billie Eilish: The World's a Little Blurry *captured many high and low moments of the singer's life. Although Eilish initially had trouble watching the film, she says she has come to appreciate it.*

An Apple Original Film

BILLIE EILISH
THE WORLD'S A LITTLE BLURRY
A FILM BY R.J. CUTLER
EXPERIENCE IT IN IMAX
FEBRUARY 26

The film shows Eilish's record company surprising her with the car, complete with a big green bow, a day before her seventeenth birthday, following an eleven-hour photo shoot for the cover of *When We All Fall Asleep, Where Do We Go?* Additional high points for Eilish shown in the film include her fan crush Justin Bieber hugging her at Coachella in 2019 after they meet for the first time and her winning multiple Grammy Awards in 2020.

The camera also documents low points for Eilish, including her bouts with Tourette's syndrome and multiple leg and ankle injuries, as well as her anguish over her 2019 performance at Coachella and her dejection when her boyfriend at the time fails her. The boy she calls "Q"—Brandon Quention Adams, a rapper who performs under the name 7:AMP—seldom appears on-screen. Mostly Eilish is seen talking with him on her smart-

Synesthesia

Billie Eilish has described the song "Everybody Dies" from her second album, *Happier Than Ever*, as blue. From her debut album, she has described "Bury a Friend" as dark colored—gray, black, brown—and "Xanny" as velvety. When she creates a piece of music, Eilish thinks about its color, shape, and texture.

Eilish's multisensory experience with music reflects her synesthesia, a perceptual phenomenon in which activation of one sense activates another at the same time. Estimates are that 3 to 5 percent of the population exhibits some form of synesthesia. Research indicates that synesthesia runs in families, which helps explain why Eilish's brother, Finneas O'Connell, also has it.

Additionally, research suggests that synesthetes, or people with synesthesia, tend to think more creatively than the general population and experience more vivid mental imagery as well. While there is no clinical diagnosis for synesthesia, tests such as the Synesthesia Battery measure the extent to which someone makes associations between senses. The associations need to be consistent over time to determine that the test taker has synesthesia. Yet because synesthesia is not widely studied, such tests may not be definitive.

phone, including pleading with him to visit her after her Coachella set. She also reveals that he was taken to the emergency room with a broken hand after punching a wall. By June 2019 she and Q had split up, and at a concert in New York City following the split, she is captured on film crying while singing "I Love You."

> "*The World's a Little Blurry* offers a glimmer of hope . . . that [Eilish], and those who come after her, will have the opportunity to share their gifts . . . without surrendering their command of themselves."[59]
>
> —Alexis Nedd, entertainment journalist

Many fans who watched *Billie Eilish: The World's a Little Blurry* speculated that the abuser Eilish sings about in "Your Power" is Q. Eilish objected, saying the song draws from different situations, and added that the documentary shows only bits of her relationship with Adams.

Most entertainment critics responded favorably to *Billie Eilish: The World's a Little Blurry.* The documentary scores high on the review-aggregation website Rotten Tomatoes, receiving 96 percent positive ratings from critics. Says Mashable's Alexis Nedd, "*The World's a Little Blurry* offers a glimmer of hope in the alluring darkness of Eilish's musical universe—the hope that she, and those who come after her, will have the opportunity to share their gifts with the world without surrendering their command of themselves."[59]

Love Letter to Los Angeles

On September 3, 2021, *Happier Than Ever: A Love Letter to Los Angeles*, a sixty-six-minute concert special, premiered on Disney+. In the special, codirected by filmmaker Robert Rodriguez and Oscar-nominated animator Patrick Osborne, Eilish sings all sixteen tracks in consecutive order from her *Happier Than Ever* album at the legendary Hollywood Bowl.

Eilish shares the film with an animated vision of herself created with the help of motion capture technology. The animated Eilish drives through Los Angeles in a silver Porsche Spyder with stops at landmarks such as the Hollywood Sign. Her odyssey through the city is intercut with Eilish performing to empty seats at the

Hollywood Bowl. As Eilish sings the next-to-the-last track, her animated self enters the venue and the two lock eyes, bringing the journey of the animated Eilish in search of the real Eilish to a satisfying conclusion.

The special's musical guests include Brazilian guitarist Romero Lubambo, who joins Finneas on keyboards, Andrew Marshall on drums, and the Los Angeles Philharmonic in backing Eilish for "Billie Bossa Nova." The Los Angeles Philharmonic also contributes backing for "My Future," "Halley's Comet," "Everybody Dies," "Therefore I Am," and "Goldwing." The Los Angeles Children's Chorus (LACC) sings with Eilish on "Goldwing." The song's a cappella introduction samples a hymn by classical composer Gustav Holst based on an ancient Hindu text. Eilish was introduced to the hymn when she sang with LACC, and for her, performing the song with the chorus felt like coming full circle.

Arguably, the film *Happier Than Ever* was made as an effort to engage fans with live performances of the songs on the album before Eilish resumed touring in 2022. Eilish has claimed that with the film she wants to celebrate her hometown. "It formed me, it made me who I am and gave me the opportunities that I got. I don't think I'd have any of the same anything if it wasn't for my hometown," she told *Good Morning America*. "I owed Los Angeles some love."[60]

Commitment to Caring

Eilish has persisted in using her voice to advocate for humanitarian and environmental causes. On September 25, 2021, she performed for a crowd of more than sixty thousand in New York City's Central Park as part of Global Citizen Live, a twenty-four-hour music festival spanning six continents. The festival is an outreach event for Global Citizen, an organization founded in 2008 with the goal of ending extreme poverty worldwide by the year 2030.

Later that year, Eilish granted the nonprofit CoralWatch permission to use "Ocean Eyes" in its social media campaign raising awareness about the threat of global climate change to the ecosystem of Australia's Great Barrier Reef.

Eilish's song "Ocean Eyes" is at the core of a social media campaign by CoralWatch, a nonprofit organization that seeks to raise awareness about the effects of climate change on Australia's Great Barrier Reef and its creatures, like these clownfish.

In 2022, for Eilish's return to touring, she partnered with REVERB, a nonprofit with a global reach. REVERB helps musicians, festivals, and venues lower the environmental impact of their shows and offer audience members information and resources on taking action for climate justice. "I think it's human to care,"[61] says Eilish.

Openness to Possibilities

On December 18, 2021, in a glowing tribute to his sister on Instagram for her twentieth birthday, Finneas praised Eilish for her talent as well as her kindness. Finneas was by her side to perform their song "Male Fantasy" just a week earlier, on the December 11 episode of *Saturday Night Live* (*SNL*). That night, Eilish served as the show's host in addition to its musical guest, one of only thirty-five musicians in *SNL*'s forty-seven-year history to pull double duty.

Her managers' belief in Eilish as more than a novelty or one-hit wonder but an artist able to sustain success in the entertainment industry is proving true. As she continues to evolve as an artist, a woman, and a caring human being, Eilish demonstrates not just staying power but also extraordinary potential.

SOURCE NOTES

Introduction: Gen Z Phenomenon

1. Quoted in Keziah Weir, "The Charming Billie Eilish," *Vanity Fair*, January 25, 2021. www.vanityfair.com.
2. Quoted in Katherine Schaffstall, "Billie Eilish and Brother Finneas Dedicate Grammy Win to 'Kids Who Are Making Music in Their Bedrooms,'" *Hollywood Reporter*, January 26, 2020. www.hollywoodreporter.com.
3. Quoted in Schaffstall, "Billie Eilish and Brother Finneas Dedicate Grammy Win to 'Kids Who Are Making Music in Their Bedrooms.'"
4. Charlie Harding, "Billie Eilish, the Neo-Goth, Chart-Topping Teenage Pop Star, Explained," Vox, August 19, 2019. www.vox.com.
5. Quoted in Joe Coscarelli, "Billie Eilish Is Not Your Typical 17-Year-Old Pop Star. Get Used to Her," *New York Times*, March 28, 2019. www.nytimes.com.
6. Quoted in Weir, "The Charming Billie Eilish."
7. Quoted in Rob Haskell, "How Billie Eilish Is Reinventing Pop Stardom," *Vogue*, February 3, 2020. www.vogue.com.
8. Megan Thee Stallion, "The 100 Most Influential People of 2021: Billie Eilish," *Time*, September 15, 2021. https://time.com.
9. Paul Zollo, "Billie Eilish's 2021 Grammy Acceptance Speech: The Greatest Ever or the Worst?," American Songwriter, April 2021. https://americansongwriter.com.

Chapter One: Bohemian Beginnings

10. Ann Powers, "Billie Eilish Is the Weird Achiever of the Year," NPR, December 10, 2019. www.npr.org.
11. Quoted in Haskell, "How Billie Eilish Is Reinventing Pop Stardom."
12. Quoted in Haskell, "How Billie Eilish Is Reinventing Pop Stardom."
13. Quoted in Haley Weiss, "Discovery: Billie Eilish," *Interview*, February 27, 2017. www.interviewmagazine.com.
14. Quoted in Jonathan Heaf, "Billie Eilish: Confessions of a Teenage Superstar," *British GQ*, June 4, 2020. www.gq-magazine.co.uk.
15. Quoted in Weiss, "Discovery."
16. Quoted in Haskell, "How Billie Eilish Is Reinventing Pop Stardom."
17. Quoted in Heaf, "Billie Eilish."
18. Quoted in Matt Medved, "Artist of the Year: Billie Eilish," *Spin*, December 23, 2019. www.spin.com.
19. Quoted in Laura Snapes, "'It's All About What Makes You Feel Good: Billie Eilish on New Music, Power Dynamics, and Her

Internet-Breaking Transformation," *British Vogue*, May 2, 2021. www.vogue.co.uk.

20. Quoted in Haskell, "How Billie Eilish Is Reinventing Pop Stardom."
21. Quoted in Haskell, "How Billie Eilish Is Reinventing Pop Stardom."
22. Quoted in Raina Douris and Kimberly Junod, "Billie Eilish on Speaking Up, Staying Hopeful and Keeping Busy During Lockdown," *World Cafe*, NPR, September 28, 2020. www.npr.org.
23. Quoted in Pharrell Williams, "V121: Billie Eilish by Pharrell Williams," *V*, August 19, 2019. www.vmagazine.com.
24. Quoted in Ariana Marsh, "How Billie Eilish's 'Ocean Eyes' Turned Her into an Overnight Sensation," *Teen Vogue*, February 24, 2017. www.teenvogue.com.
25. Quoted in Coscarelli, "Billie Eilish Is Not Your Typical 17-Year-Old Pop Star."
26. Quoted in Douris and Junod, "Billie Eilish on Speaking Up, Staying Hopeful and Keeping Busy During Lockdown."
27. Quoted in Douris and Junod, "Billie Eilish on Speaking Up, Staying Hopeful and Keeping Busy During Lockdown."
28. Quoted in Mark Savage, "Billie Eilish: Is She Pop's Best New Hope?," BBC, July 15, 2017. www.bbc.com.

Chapter Two: Dreams and Nightmares

29. Katherine Cusumano, "Meet Billie Eilish, Pop's Terrifying 15-Year-Old Prodigy," *W*, August 14, 2017. www.wmagazine.com.
30. Quoted in Estelle Tang, "Watch Billie Eilish's 'Bored' Video Now," *Elle*, June 26, 2017. www.elle.com.
31. Quoted in Ilana Kaplan, "Pop Newcomer Billie Eilish Wants to Be Sure You Never Forget Her," *Paper*, March 16, 2017. www.papermag.com.
32. Billie Eilish, *Billie Eilish*. New York: Grand Central, 2021, p. 85.
33. Lyndsey Havens, "The Best Live Shows of 2018: Billie Eilish," *Billboard*, December 14, 2018. www.billboard.com.
34. Quoted in August Brown, "Billie Eilish Isn't Stressing over the Grammies. She's Busy Worrying About the End of the World," *Los Angeles Times*, December 4, 2019. www.latimes.com.
35. Chris Willman, "Album Review: Billie Eilish's 'When We All Fall Asleep, Where Do We Go?,'" *Variety*, March 28, 2019. www.variety.com.
36. Suzy Exposito, "Billie Eilish's 'When We All Fall Asleep, Where Do We Go?' Is Noir Pop with Bite," *Rolling Stone*, March 29, 2019. www.rollingstone.com.
37. Quoted in Haskell, "How Billie Eilish Is Reinventing Pop Stardom."
38. Quoted in Madeleine Roth, "Billie Eilish's *When We All Fall Asleep, Where Do We Go?* A Complete Breakdown from Finneas O'Connell," *MTV News*, April 9, 2019. www.mtv.com.

39. Quoted in Molly Lambert, "Billie Eilish Is Calling the Shots," *Elle*, September 23, 2021. www.elle.com.
40. Quoted in Jonah Weiner, "Billie Eilish's Teenage Truths," *Rolling Stone*, February 22, 2019. www.rollingstone.com.
41. Quoted in Michel Martin, "Billie Eilish Knows What You're Afraid Of," *All Things Considered*, NPR, March 27, 2019. www.npr.org.
42. Quoted in Roth, "Billie Eilish's *When We All Fall Asleep, Where Do We Go?*"
43. Quoted in Douris and Junod, "Billie Eilish on Speaking Up, Staying Hopeful and Keeping Busy During Lockdown."

Chapter Three: Growth Factor

44. Quoted in Brittany Spanos, "Billie Eilish and the Pursuit of Happiness," *Rolling Stone*, June 17, 2021. www.rollingstone.com.
45. Quoted in Snapes, "It's All About What Makes You Feel Good."
46. Quoted in Spanos, "Billie Eilish and the Pursuit of Happiness."
47. Rob Sheffield, "Billie Eilish Refuses to Stand Still on the Heroically Honest 'Happier Than Ever,'" *Rolling Stone*, August 2, 2021. www.rollingstone.com.
48. Quoted in Heaf, "Billie Eilish."
49. Quoted in Lulu Garcia-Navarro, *Weekend Edition Sunday*, NPR, August 1, 2021. www.npr.org.
50. Quoted in Haskell, "How Billie Eilish Is Reinventing Pop Stardom."
51. Quoted in Spanos, "Billie Eilish and the Pursuit of Happiness."
52. Quoted in Martin, "Billie Eilish Knows What You're Afraid Of."
53. Quoted in Snapes, "It's All About What Makes You Feel Good."
54. Quoted in Spanos, "Billie Eilish and the Pursuit of Happiness."

Chapter Four: Power-Up

55. Quoted in Snapes, "It's All About What Makes You Feel Good."
56. Rich Juzwiak, "Review: Billie Eilish's New Photo Memoir Is Unpretentious to a Fault," *Los Angeles Times*, May 11, 2020. www.latimes.com.
57. Eilish, *Billie Eilish*, p. 7.
58. Quoted in Weir, "The Charming Billie Eilish."
59. Alexis Nedd, "'Billie Eilish: The World's a Little Blurry' Shows a Triumph over Typical Teen Stardom," Mashable, February 26, 2021. www.mashable.com.
60. Quoted in Sydney Urbanek, "Billie Eilish Relearns Her Hometown and Herself in Disney+ Film 'Happier Than Ever: A Love Letter to Los Angeles," *Billboard*, September 7, 2021. www.billboard.com.
61. Quoted in Weir, "The Charming Billie Eilish."

IMPORTANT EVENTS IN THE LIFE OF BILLIE EILISH

2001

December 18: Billie Eilish Pirate Baird O'Connell is born in Los Angeles.

2015

November 18: Eilish's brother, Finneas O'Connell, uploads a link on SoundCloud to a song he and Eilish recorded, "Ocean Eyes"; the song quickly goes viral.

2017

August 11: Darkroom releases Eilish's nine-track EP, *Don't Smile at Me*.

October 4: Eilish launches her first headlining concert tour, with dates in the United States and Canada.

2018

February 14: Eilish embarks on her first international tour, headlining performances in Europe as well as the United States and Canada.

2019

March 29: Darkroom releases Eilish's debut album, *When We All Fall Asleep, Where Do We Go?*

April 13: Eilish performs for the first time at the famed Coachella Valley Music and Arts Festival, kicking off a global tour in support of her LP.

August 26: Eilish wins MTV Video Music Awards for Best New Artist and Push Artist of the Year.

2020

January 26: Eilish wins five Grammy Awards: Best New Artist, Best Pop Vocal Album and Album of the Year (*When We All Fall Asleep, Where Do We Go?*), and Record of the Year and Song of the Year ("Bad Guy").

February 14: "No Time to Die," the theme song written by Eilish and Finneas for the James Bond film of the same name, is released.

2021

February 26: *Billie Eilish: The World's a Little Blurry*, a documentary film featuring Eilish, is released in theaters and on Apple TV+.

March 14: Eilish wins a Grammy Award for Record of the Year ("Everything I Wanted") and for Best Song Written for Visual Media ("No Time to Die").

July 30: Darkroom releases Eilish's sophomore album, *Happier Than Ever*.

September 12: Eilish's video for "Your Power," which she directed, wins an MTV Video Music Award for Video for Good.

September 15: *Time* magazine announces that Eilish is one of its 100 Most Influential People of 2021 and will be one of the seven honorees appearing on covers of the magazine.

2022

February 3: Eilish starts her *Happier Than Ever* world tour in New Orleans, Louisiana.

Books

Adrian Besley, *Billie Eilish: From E-girl to Icon: The Unofficial Biography*. Minneapolis, MN: Zest, 2021.

Billie Eilish, *Billie Eilish*. New York: Grand Central, 2021.

Stuart Kallen, *Stand Up Against Climate Change*. San Diego, CA: ReferencePoint, 2022.

Saddleback Educational Publishing, *Billie Eilish/Halsey*. Costa Mesa, CA: Saddleback Educational, 2020.

Jennifer Stephen, *Stand Up for Animal Welfare*. San Diego, CA: ReferencePoint, 2022.

Internet Sources

August Brown, "Billie Eilish Isn't Stressing over the Grammies. She's Busy Worrying About the End of the World," *Los Angeles Times*, December 4, 2019. www.latimes.com.

Rob Haskell, "How Billie Eilish Is Reinventing Pop Stardom," *Vogue*, February 3, 2020. www.vogue.com.

Matt Medved, "Artist of the Year: Billie Eilish," *Spin*, December 23, 2019. www.spin.com.

Laura Snapes, "It's All About What Makes You Feel Good: Billie Eilish on New Music, Power Dynamics, and Her Internet-Breaking Transformation," *British Vogue*, May 2, 2021. www.vogue.co.uk.

Brittany Spanos, "Billie Eilish and the Pursuit of Happiness," *Rolling Stone*, June 17, 2021. www.rollingstone.com.

Keziah Weir, "The Charming Billie Eilish," *Vanity Fair*, January 25, 2021. www.vanityfair.com.

Haley Weiss, "Discovery: Billie Eilish," *Interview*, February 27, 2017. www.interviewmagazine.com.

INDEX

PICTURE CREDITS

Cover: Cubankite/Shutterstock.com

6: UPI/Alamy Stock Photo

10: Maks Ershov/Shutterstock.com

13: Ben Houdijk/Shutterstock.com

17: Christian Bertrand/Shutterstock.com

20: Photofest Images

25: Erin Cardigan/Alamy Stock Photo

29: Associated Press

33: Associated Press

34: Kathy deWitt/Alamy Stock Photo

39: Silvia Elizabeth Pangaro/Shutterstock.com

45: UPI/Alamy Stock Photo

49: BFA/Alamy Stock Photo

53: MaxPalla/Shutterstock.com

ABOUT THE AUTHOR

Amy Allison has authored five biographies for young people. Her short fiction appears at RoseCitySisters.com and New-Myths.com. She has also written a novel spotlighting the 1960s music scene on the Sunset Strip in Los Angeles, where she now lives.